I0012276

Mind in Motion: AI Robotics for the Curious Creator

M.S. Ali

Published by Desert Particle, 2025.

MIND IN MOTION: AI ROBOTICS FOR THE CURIOUS CREATOR

First edition. April 4, 2025.

Written by M.S. Ali.

Also by M.S. Ali

Celestial Wonders
Celestial Secrets - Unlocking the Universe
Our Cosmic Neighborhood - A Tour of Our Galactic Backyard
Beyond the Visible: The Search for Dark Matter
Quantum Curiosities: A Journey Into the Heart of the Quantum World

Wonders of Chemistry
The Green Chemistry Revolution: The Way to a Sustainable Future to a
Sustainable Future

Standalone
AI and the Future: The Algorithmic Age
Quantum Computing for All
The Kitchen Alchemist: The Science of Flavor
Dust to Efficiency: Optimizing Baghouse Operations in Limestone
Calcining
Earth's Tipping Point: Navigating the Anthropocene
The Rise of Autonomous AI: AI's new Dawn
Mind in Motion: AI Robotics for the Curious Creator

Watch for more at desertparticle.com.

Table of Contents

Mind in Motion: AI Robotics for the curious creator

About the Author

M.S. ALI IS AN ESTEEMED science and technology enthusiast, celebrated for transforming intricate scientific concepts into engaging narratives that resonate with both laypersons and experts alike. With a unique voice that blends clarity and creativity, Ali has dedicated their career to demystifying the rapidly evolving world of artificial intelligence and robotics. By synthesizing extensive research through the lens of accessible storytelling, Ali has established themselves as a trusted figure in the field, creating fascinating works that maintain scientific integrity while captivating diverse audiences.

With a solid foundation in both practice and theory, Ali has amassed extensive experience in various sectors of science and technology. Their professional journey includes roles as a consultant and speaker, where they have influenced both emerging innovators and seasoned professionals. Engaging in collaborative projects with universities and technology firms, Ali has gained unique insights into the latest trends and breakthroughs, positioning them as an authoritative voice on AI and robotics. This hands-on experience not only enriches their writing but also provides readers with a grounded perspective on technology's impact on society.

Ali's academic background in engineering and computer science has been instrumental in shaping their analytical approach to writing. Their education has equipped them with the tools to dissect complex ideas and present them in a manner that is both engaging and comprehensible. The journey as a writer began with a fervent desire to share knowledge and spark curiosity about technology. Through previous publications, Ali has honed their ability to engage readers, creating works that inspire critical thinking and encourage exploration in the fields of AI and robotics.

Beyond their academic prowess, Ali's personal journey reflects a deep-seated passion for innovation and creativity. Their writing style is characterized by a conversational tone that invites readers on a journey through the captivating world of technology. By interweaving personal anecdotes and relatable examples, Ali crafts stories that resonate with the audience, making complex ideas feel approachable and relevant. This commitment to accessibility not only solidifies their connection with readers but also reflects their belief that knowledge should be shared freely and creatively.

As a dedicated author, Ali's mission is to bridge the gap between complex scientific themes and public understanding, fostering a sense of curiosity and engagement with new technologies. Looking ahead, Ali aims to continue exploring the intersections of AI and creativity while empowering others to innovate within this transformative field. Through their writing and outreach, Ali aspires to inspire a new generation of thinkers and creators, ensuring that the wonders of technology are within reach for everyone.

Table of Contents

Chapter 1: Introduction to AI Robotics

Chapter 2: Foundations of Artificial Intelligence

Robotics

Chapter 15: Community and Collaboration in AI Robotics

Chapter 1: Introduction to AI Robotics

1.1 The Evolution of Robotics and AI

THE JOURNEY OF ROBOTICS and artificial intelligence is a fascinating tapestry woven from various historical milestones. One of the earliest significant developments can be traced back to ancient civilizations, where myths and legends spoke of mechanical beings and automatons that served humans. Fast forward to the 20th century, and we see the birth of modern robotics marked by the introduction of the first industrial robot, Unimate, in 1961. This pivotal moment set the stage for a new era where machines began to take on tasks in manufacturing, performing repetitive and dangerous tasks to increase efficiency and safety. The subsequent decades witnessed rapid advancements in technology, leading to the establishment of algorithms that allowed machines to learn from data and adapt to their environments. The invention of the microprocessor in the 1970s further catalyzed developments, making it possible for machines to process information at unprecedented speeds. Continuing through the late 20th century and into the 21st, milestones such as the development of deep learning and neural networks revolutionized how machines perceive and interact with the world, leading to the creation of systems that can recognize faces, understand languages, and even drive cars autonomously.

Throughout this evolution, several key figures have played pivotal roles in the advancement of robotics and artificial intelligence. Notable among them is Alan Turing, whose groundbreaking work laid the mathematical foundation of computer science and proposed the concept of a universal machine, essential for both robotics and AI. His Turing Test remains a benchmark for assessing a machine's ability to exhibit intelligent behavior equivalent to that of a human. Another influential figure, Norbert Wiener, is often regarded as the father of cybernetics, which contributed significantly to understanding the feedback loops in intelligent systems. The invention of various robotic devices can also be attributed to many innovators, including George Devol, who created the first programmable robot, and Rodney Brooks, known for his contributions to behavior-based robotics. Innovations such as AI that can recognize patterns or make decisions autonomously have reshaped industries ranging from healthcare to finance. These advancements illustrate a trajectory, not only characterized by technological progress but also by philosophical debates on the implications of machines becoming increasingly autonomous and intelligent.

In contemplating the future of robotics and AI, technology enthusiasts should remember that today's innovations are merely stepping stones toward a more integrated relationship between humans and machines. As we explore recent advancements, such as the use of robotics in remote surgery or AI-driven personalized learning, it remains crucial to consider the ethical implications and responsibilities that come with these technologies. Understanding both the historical context and the contributions of key figures can provide valuable insights into not just where robotics and AI have been, but also where they are heading. Engaging with these ideas can enhance one's appreciation for the complexity of this field and inspire curiosity about future possibilities.

Keep an eye on emerging developments and consider how they might shape your understanding of technology.

1.2 Defining AI Robotics: Concepts and Terminology

UNDERSTANDING THE ESSENTIAL terms surrounding artificial intelligence (AI) and robotics is crucial for technology enthusiasts. Vocabulary such as robot, automation, machine learning, and intelligence often intertwines, yet each holds distinct meanings. A robot is typically defined as a programmable machine capable of carrying out a series of tasks automatically. Automation refers to the use of technology to perform tasks without human intervention, and it can act as a stepping stone in the development of autonomous robots. Machine learning, a subset of AI, focuses on the ability of systems to learn from data and improve their performance over time without being explicitly programmed. By clarifying these terms, enthusiasts can foster a common understanding that is essential for deeper engagement with the field of AI robotics.

The interdisciplinary nature of AI robotics is one of its most fascinating aspects. This field is not confined to a single area of study; instead, it resides at the crossroads of engineering, computer science, and cognitive studies. Engineers design and build the physical bodies of robots, while computer scientists develop the software that enables these machines to function intelligently. Cognitive studies contribute insights into how humans think and learn, which can inform the design of AI systems. Understanding how these disciplines intersect enhances our appreciation of the complexity and potential of AI robotics, as it empowers individuals to think creatively about merging different skills and knowledge areas to solve complex problems. For those interested in the field, exploring these connections can lead to innovative applications and inspire collaborative projects that reflect the dynamic nature of AI robotics.

As you delve deeper into AI robotics, consider keeping abreast of the latest developments by following technological trends and research. This will not only enrich your understanding but also inspire new ideas and applications. Engaging with communities of like-minded enthusiasts can provide additional perspectives and foster collaborative exploration of this exciting domain.

1.3 Importance of AI Robotics in Modern Technology

THE TRANSFORMATIVE impact of AI robotics on various sectors has become increasingly evident in recent years. Industries like manufacturing, healthcare, and logistics have seen significant advancements due to the integration of robotic systems powered by artificial intelligence. In manufacturing, robots are taking over repetitive tasks, which not only speeds up production but also reduces human error. These machines can operate around the clock, maintaining a level of precision that is challenging for human workers to match. In healthcare, robotic surgery has revolutionized procedures, enabling surgeons to perform complex operations with enhanced dexterity and less invasiveness. This leads to quicker recovery times for patients and fewer complications.

Moreover, AI robotics is beginning to influence everyday life in profound ways. The emergence of smart home devices and personal assistants powered by AI is changing how people interact with technology on a daily basis. These tools learn from user behavior and preferences, making them increasingly intuitive and effective at helping with everyday tasks, from managing schedules to controlling household appliances. This not only enhances convenience but also fosters a more interconnected lifestyle where technology seamlessly integrates into personal routines.

The potential of AI robotics to solve complex challenges is vast, offering solutions that improve efficiency and productivity across diverse fields. For instance, in agriculture, robotic systems equipped with AI can analyze soil health and optimize planting strategies, leading to higher crop yields and sustainable farming practices. In transportation, autonomous vehicles are being developed to reduce traffic accidents and improve traffic flow. These advancements not only promise to minimize human error but also address pressing issues like congestion and environmental concerns. As organizations adopt these technologies, they find that not only do they save time and costs, but they are also able to reallocate human resources to more creative and strategic tasks, amplifying overall productivity.

Understanding the significance of AI robotics in modern technology highlights the potential for innovation that can change the fabric of society. The ability of these systems to analyze vast amounts of data and execute tasks with minimal supervision creates an exciting opportunity for the future. Technology enthusiasts should consider exploring the advancements in AI robotics continually, as they will undoubtedly shape the subsequent evolution of industries and daily life. Keeping abreast of these technological shifts can provide invaluable insights that could lead to personal and professional growth in an increasingly automated world.

Chapter 2: Foundations of Artificial Intelligence

2.1 Overview of AI: History and Milestones

THE JOURNEY OF ARTIFICIAL intelligence (AI) stretches back to the mid-20th century, a time when the seeds of computational thought were first sown. In 1950, Alan Turing proposed the Turing Test, a criterion of intelligence that focused on a machine's ability to exhibit human-like behavior. This early conceptual framework laid the groundwork for subsequent research and exploration. Fast forward to the 1956 Dartmouth Conference, where John McCarthy and his peers coined the term artificial intelligence, marking a significant milestone that united various strands of scientific inquiry under this nascent field.

Throughout the 1960s and 1970s, developments such as the creation of early neural networks and natural language processing systems sparked initial enthusiasm and laid the foundation for further innovations.

The evolution of AI witnessed several cycles of optimism and retreat, often referred to as 'AI winters', periods when funding and interest waned due to unmet expectations. However, significant breakthroughs emerged from these lulls, especially in the late 1990s and early 2000s. The introduction of machine learning algorithms that improved through experience and the revival of neural networks, particularly with deep learning, led to revolutionary capabilities in image and speech recognition. Today, AI stands at the forefront of technological advancement, driven by vast amounts of data and powerful computational resources. Its applications now permeate sectors such as healthcare, finance, and transportation, showcasing a transformative potential that was unimaginable a few decades ago. This era marks AI not only as a field rich in complexity but also as an integral part of societal evolution.

AI's positioning as a frontier technology of the 21st century can largely be attributed to key developments that reflect growing sophistication and applicability. One major leap was the success of IBM's Watson in 2011, which demonstrated the power of machine learning in a real-world application by winning the quiz show Jeopardy! This high-profile success captured public imagination and sparked interest among industries looking for competitive advantages. Additionally, the development of autonomous systems, such as self-driving cars and drones, showcases AI's ability to redefine typical operational frameworks, pushing boundaries in efficiency and safety. The proliferation of smart assistants like Siri and Alexa indicates broader consumer acceptance of AI technology in everyday life. As we continue to innovate, the philosophical implications of AI also demand attention, prompting discussions on ethics, machine rights, and the very essence of intelligence. Engaging with these concepts not only informs technological advancement but also shapes the future societal landscape.

2.2 Machine Learning vs. Traditional Programming

THE PRINCIPLES OF MACHINE learning starkly contrast with those of traditional programming models. Traditional programming is based on a straightforward paradigm: developers write explicit rules and instructions for computers to follow. In this method, every possible scenario must be anticipated and coded directly into the program. The computer's performance in executing these rules is entirely dependent on the accuracy and completeness of the instructions provided by the programmer. This deterministic nature means that the outcome is predictable; input a specific command, and the program will unfailingly produce the same result each time. However, this approach becomes increasingly complex when faced with an array of uncertain or variable data. Here, the limitations of traditional programming become evident, as it lacks the flexibility to adapt to new and unforeseen circumstances.

Machine learning, on the other hand, offers a transformative method of programming where systems learn and adapt through experience. Rather than relying solely on hard-coded rules, machine learning algorithms identify patterns in data and use those insights to make decisions or predictions. This form of programming enables systems to improve over time as they process more information, effectively allowing them to refine their knowledge and increase accuracy autonomously. For example, a machine learning model can analyze thousands, if not millions, of data points to discern trends and anomalies that a traditional program would struggle to encapsulate within fixed rules. Each iteration of training increases its proficiency, leading to a continually evolving capability that adjusts to new data inputs seamlessly. The adaptability inherent in machine learning stands as a pillar of its innovation, marking a significant departure from the static nature of conventional programming methods.

Ultimately, the essential difference lies in the approach to problem-solving and system functionality. Traditional programming offers control and predictability with a rigid structure, while machine learning embodies fluidity and self-improvement, showcasing the incredible potential of systems that can learn from their surroundings. Understanding these differences is vital for technology enthusiasts; as we venture further into an era dominated by artificial intelligence and big data, recognizing when to leverage traditional methods versus embracing the learning capabilities of machine learning can lead to more effective and innovative solutions.

2.3 Key Algorithms and Computational Models in AI

UNDERSTANDING THE FOUNDATIONAL algorithms that drive modern AI applications is crucial for grasping how artificial intelligence operates in practice. Decision trees, for instance, are among the simplest yet most effective algorithms for classification tasks. They work by splitting the dataset into branches based on feature values, making decisions at each node until a final classification is reached. This tree-like structure allows for easy interpretation, visualizing decisions much like a flowchart. In contrast, neural networks mimic the structure of the human brain, composed of interconnected nodes or neurons. Each neuron processes input data, applying weights and biases to recognize patterns, learning through both supervised and unsupervised training methods. These algorithms, while fundamentally different in approach, showcase the diverse pathways that AI can take to analyze data and derive meaningful insights.

The computational models that form the backbone of AI facilitate an array of tasks integral to processing complex datasets. One notable model is the support vector machine (SVM), which excels in finding the optimal hyperplane that separates data points of different classes. This is especially useful in tasks involving high-dimensional spaces, where visualizing the data is not feasible. Moreover, clustering algorithms, such as k-means and hierarchical clustering, assist in organizing unlabeled data into meaningful groups. These models enable AI systems to recognize patterns without prior knowledge, allowing for exploratory data analysis that can reveal hidden structures within the data. Such models empower machines to learn from raw data, translating it into actionable knowledge.

To effectively engage with AI, a solid understanding of these algorithms and models is essential. Experimentation is the key to mastering their application. Resources such as open-source libraries allow technology enthusiasts to implement various algorithms and observe their performance on diverse datasets. Engaging in hands-on projects can deepen this understanding and expand one's ability to leverage AI in innovative ways, potentially leading to breakthroughs in how we interact with technology.

Chapter 3: Robotics Fundamentals

3.1 Types of Robots: Industrial, Service, and Social

ROBOTS ARE CATEGORIZED based on their applications, functionality, and environment. Industrial robots are primarily designed for manufacturing tasks. These machines excel in repetitive tasks such as welding, painting, assembly, and material handling. For example, automotive assembly lines utilize robotic arms to perform precise painting and assembly operations, greatly increasing efficiency and safety. Service robots, on the other hand, are designed to assist humans in tasks outside industrial environments. They include robots that perform cleaning duties, like robotic vacuum cleaners, and those employed in healthcare settings for tasks such as patient monitoring or drug dispensing. Social robots are a more recent category that focuses on interacting with humans in a social context. These robots, like Pepper or Sophia, are built to understand and respond to human emotions, making them suitable for companionship or customer service roles.

The roles of robots in society are evolving rapidly, impacting various aspects of our daily lives. Initially seen as tools for automation in factories, robots have transformed industries by enhancing productivity and precision while reducing human error. Modern factories leverage collaborative robots, or cobots, that work alongside human operators, enhancing efficiency through teamwork. In the realm of personal life, robots are transitioning from mere functional devices to companions that can mitigate loneliness and provide emotional support. For instance, in households, pet-like robots are becoming increasingly popular, offering companionship and entertainment. This shift indicates a deeper integration of robots into our societal fabric, portraying them as entities that can enhance the quality of life rather than just mechanized tools. Understanding this transformation can inspire technology enthusiasts to explore innovative applications that extend beyond traditional uses.

As technology continues to advance, it is vital to consider the ethical implications of integrating robots into our daily lives. Proactively engaging with the potential societal impacts of robotics can pave the way for a future where humans and robots coexist harmoniously, improving productivity and emotional wellbeing alike. Keeping an eye on these advancements will empower you to engage with and shape the narrative around robotic technologies.

3.2 Basic Components of a Robotics System

A ROBOTIC SYSTEM IS built upon several essential components that work in concert to enable machines to execute a range of tasks. The most fundamental of these components are sensors, actuators, and controllers. Sensors serve as the eyes and ears of a robot, gathering information from the environment, which can include light, temperature, distance, and even sounds. These sensors convert physical phenomena into signals that can be interpreted by the robot's control system. For instance, a proximity sensor can determine how close an object is, while a camera might capture images that the robot then analyzes to make decisions about navigating its surroundings.

Actuators are the muscles of the robotic system, transforming the electrical signals generated by the controllers into physical movement. They can be motors, servos, or hydraulic systems, responsible for the robot's actions such as moving arms, wheels, or legs. When a controller receives information from the sensors, it processes this data and determines the appropriate response, sending signals to the actuators to execute the desired motion. Controllers are essentially the brain of the robot, running algorithms and making decisions based on sensor input. They interpret signals and deduce the best course of action, creating a seamless flow of information that allows robots to operate effectively and adaptively in their environments.

This synergy between sensors, actuators, and controllers illustrates the remarkable capability of robots to perceive and interact with their surroundings. For example, in an autonomous vehicle, a combination of camera sensors and Lidar technology allows the vehicle to map its environment, while a sophisticated control system processes this data to steer and adjust speed, ensuring safe navigation. Understanding how these components function together enhances our appreciation of robotic technology and its potential. As you dive deeper into robotics, consider experimenting with simple sensors and actuators to build your own robotic prototypes, as hands-on experience can reveal the intricacies of these fundamental elements.

3.3 Sensor Technologies in Robotics

VARIOUS SENSOR TECHNOLOGIES play a crucial role in the realm of robotics, as they enable machines to perceive and interpret the world around them. Sensors like ultrasonic, infrared, and tactile sensors allow robots to detect distance, obstacles, and surfaces, enabling them to navigate with precision. Each type of sensor provides unique input, which is essential for machine learning algorithms that help robots understand their environments. For instance, tactile sensors enable robots to handle objects delicately and perform tasks that require a human-like sense of touch. As robotics technology advances, the integration of these sensors allows for smarter, more responsive robots that can adapt to varying situations. The ability to perceive surroundings not only enhances the functionality of robots but also broadens their applications in industries ranging from manufacturing to healthcare.

Recent advancements in sensor technologies such as LiDAR (Light Detection and Ranging) and high-resolution cameras have significantly transformed the capabilities of robotics. LiDAR has become a game-changer by providing precise, three-dimensional mapping of environments, allowing robots to navigate complex terrains and avoid obstacles with remarkable accuracy. This technology is particularly useful in applications like autonomous vehicles and drones, where understanding spatial relationships is critical. Similarly, advancements in camera technology, including stereo vision and depth perception, enable robots to gain insights comparable to human vision. These enhanced visual systems facilitate advanced tasks, such as object recognition and scene understanding, which are vital for autonomous decision-making. As these sensor technologies continue to evolve, they present an exciting frontier for innovation in robotics, fostering developments that amplify both functionality and safety.

As a practical tip for technology enthusiasts, exploring DIY robotics projects that incorporate various sensors can provide hands-on experience with these technologies. Building your own robotic systems allows for experimentation with different sensors, enhancing your understanding of their capabilities and limitations. This experience can prove invaluable as you delve deeper into the fascinating world of robotics.

Chapter 4: The Intersection of AI and Robotics

4.1 How AI Enhances Robotic Functionality

AI ALGORITHMS SIGNIFICANTLY enhance the decision-making capabilities of robots by enabling them to process and analyze vast amounts of data quickly and accurately. These algorithms allow robots to learn from their environment in real-time, leading to better predictions and smarter actions. For instance, through machine learning techniques, robots can identify patterns and adapt to new situations without requiring explicit programming for every possible scenario. This is especially valuable in dynamic environments where conditions frequently change, such as warehouses or disaster response scenes. By leveraging neural networks, robots can categorize objects, understand their surroundings, and make informed choices based on previous experiences, thereby improving their operational efficiency and effectiveness.

The integration of AI into robotic systems leads to remarkable advancements in autonomy and efficiency across various applications. In manufacturing, for instance, AI-powered robots can autonomously adjust their workflows based on real-time production data, optimizing output and reducing waste. Similarly, in agriculture, drones equipped with AI can monitor crop health and provide targeted interventions, thus boosting yield while minimizing resource use. In healthcare, robotic surgical systems that utilize AI can assist surgeons by providing critical insights during procedures, enhancing precision and reducing recovery times for patients. The ability of these intelligent systems to function without constant human oversight exemplifies how AI is driving the next level of robotic autonomy, allowing for faster and more efficient operations across diverse fields.

The implications of AI-enhanced robotic functionality extend beyond just improved efficiency; they also raise philosophical questions about the future of work and human-robot collaboration. As robots become more autonomous and capable, they are likely to take on tasks that were traditionally performed by humans, which can lead to transformative changes in various industries. This shift necessitates a deeper understanding of how to integrate these technologies responsibly and ethically into society. Embracing this technology invites us to rethink not only how we approach automation, but also how we can leverage it to enhance human capabilities rather than replace them. It is essential to foster a symbiotic relationship where AI and robotics augment human efforts, leading to a future rich with possibilities for innovation and growth.

4.2 Case Studies: Successful AI Robotics Applications

SEVERAL INDUSTRIES have successfully integrated AI robotics into their operations, showcasing the transformative power of this technology. In the manufacturing sector, companies like Tesla have utilized AI-driven robots for assembling vehicles. This not only enhances precision in the production process but also significantly boosts efficiency. Another notable example is the healthcare industry, where robotic systems, such as the da Vinci Surgical System, assist surgeons in performing minimally invasive surgeries with greater accuracy and reduced recovery times. In agriculture, autonomous drones are being employed for monitoring crop health and optimizing pesticide application, illustrating how AI can enhance food production sustainability and efficiency.

These success stories reveal crucial lessons about implementing AI robotics. One important takeaway is the necessity of robust training data to ensure that AI systems are accurate and reliable. In Tesla's case, the massive amounts of data collected from its vehicles allow its robots to adapt and learn, improving over time. Moreover, collaboration between human workers and robotic systems has proven essential. Facilities that foster a culture of teamwork between humans and robots tend to achieve higher productivity levels and better job satisfaction. This highlights the need for organizations to invest not only in technology but also in their workforce's skills and perspectives, ensuring that humans and machines can work harmoniously.

The impact of these implementations extends beyond just operational improvements; they also initiate shifts in workforce dynamics and drive the evolution of industry standards. Robotics technology prompts a re-evaluation of roles within companies, pushing workers to adapt and learn new skills. To stay competitive, businesses must embrace continuous learning and integration of advanced technologies. As industries evolve, so too should the strategies for workforce development, emphasizing the importance of training programs that focus on human-robot collaboration. If a business leverages the strengths of both AI and its human workforce, it can not only enhance productivity but also create an innovative environment resilient to future changes.

4.3 Ethical Considerations in AI-Driven Robotics

THE DEPLOYMENT OF AI-driven robotics introduces a host of ethical dilemmas that warrant careful examination. These advanced systems have the potential to transform industries, enhance productivity, and improve quality of life. However, they also raise significant questions about privacy, autonomy, and accountability. For instance, when robots make decisions in critical areas such as healthcare or law enforcement, the stakes are incredibly high. Who is responsible when a robot malfunctions or makes a harmful decision? This uncertainty poses a dilemma: while societies benefit from innovations in robotics, they must also navigate the risks associated with reliance on machines that lack human intuition and moral judgment. Moreover, the fear of job displacement caused by automation may exacerbate social inequalities, leading to a more divided society. Hence, the discussions surrounding the ethical implications of AI-driven robotics are not just theoretical; they are crucial for ensuring that technological advancements serve humanity as a whole.

Establishing ethical guidelines is essential to secure responsible AI development and deployment. These guidelines provide a framework that can assist developers and organizations in making informed decisions about the design and application of robotic systems. They should encompass principles such as transparency, fairness, accountability, and respect for human rights. For example, transparency in how AI algorithms operate can help build trust among users, while fairness ensures that these technologies serve diverse populations equitably, rather than perpetuating existing biases. Furthermore, accountability is vital; stakeholders need clarity on who is liable when a robot's actions lead to unintended consequences. Incorporating these ethical principles from the outset can foster a culture of responsibility in tech development, enabling innovations that honor the rights and dignity of individuals.

As technology enthusiasts, understanding these ethical considerations is imperative. Engaging with the broader conversations around AI ethics not only enhances your knowledge but also positions you as a part of the ongoing dialogue that shapes the future of technology. To contribute meaningfully, consider exploring relevant frameworks and case studies that illustrate the successes and failures of ethical decision-making in AI-driven robotics. By being informed and proactive, you can help shape a future where technology and ethics align harmoniously.

Chapter 5: Designing Intelligent Robots

5.1 Principles of Robot Design

THE DESIGN PROCESS of intelligent robots is guided by a set of fundamental principles that ensure functionality, efficiency, and adaptability. At the core of these principles lies the concept of purpose-driven design, which means that every aspect of a robot must align with its intended task. From the selection of materials to the choice of sensors and motors, each decision influences how effectively a robot can perform its duties. Additionally, human-robot interaction is a critical consideration; user-friendly interfaces and intuitive controls can significantly enhance the robot's utility and user adoption. Furthermore, the principle of modularity allows for flexibility, enabling designers to create robots that can be easily upgraded or modified depending on evolving needs or technologies. The balance between complexity and simplicity is another essential aspect, as overly complex systems may introduce failure points while simple designs can lack adaptability.

Examining case studies of innovative robot designs provides insights into how these principles have been effectively implemented to tackle specific challenges. For instance, Boston Dynamics' Spot robot exemplifies a design that prioritizes mobility and versatility in diverse terrains, fulfilling roles in security, construction, and even healthcare settings. Its modular design incorporates various payload configurations which can change based on the task at hand. Another notable example is Soft Robotics' grippers, which utilize soft materials to handle fragile objects, demonstrating an application of human-inspired design principles that enhance interaction with various items while minimizing damage. These designs showcase how creativity and practicality converge to create robots that meet real-world needs, proving that thoughtful application of design principles can result in groundbreaking innovations.

As the field of robotics continues to evolve, staying informed about new materials, algorithms, and technologies is crucial for aspiring designers. This continuous learning mindset will enable them to push the boundaries of what robots can achieve, guiding them through the complexity of design challenges while keeping the principles of ergonomic design and functionality in focus.

5.2 Integrating AI into Robotic Systems

INTEGRATING AI CAPABILITIES into robotic systems involves a careful blend of various methodologies tailored to enhance functionality. One prevalent approach is using machine learning algorithms that allow robots to analyze and learn from their environments. This is achieved through techniques such as reinforcement learning, where robots are trained to make decisions based on feedback from their actions, improving their performance over time. Computer vision is another critical element, enabling robots to interpret visual information and navigate their surroundings intelligently. The deployment of natural language processing facilitates seamless human-robot interaction, making it possible for robots to understand and respond to voice commands, thus enhancing usability. Moreover, sensor fusion techniques combine data from multiple sensors, allowing for richer and more comprehensive environmental awareness. Integrating these AI capabilities transforms conventional machines into intelligent entities capable of decision-making, problem-solving, and complex task execution.

The fusion of mechanical design and AI intelligence stands as a cornerstone for developing more autonomous robots. This integration begins at the design phase, where engineers create structures optimized for the specific tasks the robot will engage in, considering both physical capabilities and cognitive functions. Advanced materials and flexible structures are often employed to allow robots greater adaptability in various environments. By incorporating AI, robots can learn to modify their behavior based on real-time data, enhancing their autonomy. For instance, a robotic arm equipped with AI can learn the intricacies of tasks like assembly or precision placement, adjusting its movements to improve efficiency and accuracy. The interplay of these elements leads to the emergence of robots that not only perform predefined tasks but also exhibit a degree of learning and adaptability; traits that were once thought to be uniquely human. Through continued research and innovation, future robots promise a level of autonomy that allows them to operate in dynamic environments with minimal human intervention.

Understanding the relationship between mechanical design and AI opens doors to a new realm of possibilities in robotics. Those interested in this field should stay informed about advancements in both AI technologies and mechanical engineering. The integration of these disciplines is an ongoing journey, where breakthroughs in one area can lead to innovative solutions in another, often in unexpected ways. Remaining curious and open to learning helps enthusiasts not only grasp the current landscape but also participate actively in shaping the future of intelligent robotic systems.

5.3 Prototyping and Testing Intelligent Robots

THE PROTOTYPING PROCESS is a foundational stage in the development of intelligent robots, allowing engineers and designers to explore ideas and translate abstract concepts into tangible objects. It provides a unique opportunity to identify challenges early in the design life cycle, minimizing costly modifications at later stages. Prototyping is not just about creating a functional robot; it encompasses the essence of experimentation and innovation. By developing initial models, developers can test hypotheses about the robot's behaviors, functionalities, and interactions with its environment. This iterative process encourages continuous improvement, where feedback from each prototype iteration refines both design and functionality. Early simulations and modifications based on testing results establish a feedback loop that is indispensable for achieving a high-performance final product. Prototyping, therefore, is not merely a step in the development process but a dynamic tool that bridges creativity with practicality, fostering a deeper understanding of both technology and user needs.

The methodologies employed in testing robotic systems are crucial for ensuring their performance and reliability in real-world applications. Testing involves several approaches, including functionality testing, stress testing, and user acceptance testing, each designed to unveil different aspects of a robot's capabilities. Functionality testing ensures every component operates as intended, verifying that sensors respond accurately and that movement is fluid and reliable. Stress testing assesses how well a robot can perform under extreme conditions, such as varied temperatures or unexpected obstacles, which is critical to understanding a robot's limits. User acceptance testing brings in real-world users to interact with the robot, gathering invaluable insights about usability and ensuring that the design meets the anticipated needs of its target audience. By combining quantitative data from performance metrics with qualitative feedback from users, developers can create more nuanced assessments of their robots, leading to innovations that truly resonate with human users. Each of these testing methods plays a significant role in confirming that robotic systems not only function as intended but also inspire trust and confidence in their users.

Chapter 6: Programming Robots with AI

6.1 Programming Languages for Robotics Development

ROBOTICS DEVELOPMENT encompasses a variety of programming languages, each offering distinct features that cater to different aspects of robotics. Among the most popular languages are C++, Python, and Java. C++ is revered for its performance and control over system resources, enabling developers to write efficient code crucial for real-time tasks in robotics, such as controlling motors and processing sensor data. Its object-oriented features also promote code reusability, making it a preferred choice for complex robotic systems. Python, on the other hand, attracts developers for its simplicity and readability, allowing for quick prototyping and rapid development. It is highly favored in educational settings and research due to extensive libraries like ROSPy for Robot Operating System integration and OpenCV for computer vision. Java provides platform independence and a strong ecosystem, which is particularly beneficial in large-scale robotic applications and systems that require interoperability. The language's built-in garbage collection also helps in managing memory, an essential factor in long-running robotic applications.

When selecting a programming language for robotics projects, developers must navigate a set of trade-offs. Performance requirements often clash with ease of development. For instance, while C++ allows for fine-tuning in resource-constrained environments, it has a steeper learning curve and can lead to longer development times compared to Python. Stability and maintainability also come into play; languages with a strong community and rich libraries may offer more support over time but could lag in performance compared to lower-level languages. Therefore, considerations such as the project's scope, team expertise, and specific application requirements must guide the choice of language. Many engineers opt to use a combination, employing C++ for performance-critical components while leveraging Python for higher-level logic and interface development. This hybrid approach can harness the strengths of multiple languages, though it may introduce additional complexity in integration and dependencies.

Awareness of these programming languages and their respective strengths and weaknesses can greatly enhance the effectiveness of robotics developers. A practical tip for those venturing into robotics programming is to start small, perhaps with Python for rapid prototyping, before gradually tackling performance issues that may arise in more complex applications requiring C++. This strategy allows for a gradual learning curve, providing a solid foundation in both coding and robotics concepts while fostering an understanding of when to leverage the unique capabilities of each language.

6.2 Implementing Machine Learning in Robotics

INTEGRATING MACHINE learning algorithms into robotics programming represents a transformative advancement in how robots perceive and interact with their environments. Various approaches exist to facilitate this integration, often tailored to the specific needs of the robot's tasks. One prominent method is reinforcement learning, where robots learn optimal actions through trial and error while receiving feedback from their surroundings. This technique is especially useful in dynamic environments where tasks may change, allowing robots to adapt by continually refining their strategies based on the outcomes of their actions. Another approach is supervised learning, where robots are trained on vast datasets to recognize patterns and make predictions. By exposing robots to numerous examples, they learn to make informed decisions in real-time, enhancing their ability to navigate complex environments and perform intricate tasks. The effectiveness of machine learning in robotics can be observed across various real-world applications, demonstrating significant improvements in performance. In manufacturing, for instance, robots equipped with machine learning capabilities can predict equipment failures, optimizing maintenance schedules and reducing downtime. These predictive capabilities enable companies to keep production lines running smoothly while minimizing costs. In the realm of autonomous vehicles, machine learning algorithms process sensor data to enhance object recognition and anticipation of driver behavior. This leads to safer navigation in unpredictable traffic scenarios, showcasing the potential of machine learning to elevate robot functionality. Furthermore, in healthcare, robots utilizing machine learning can assist in surgeries by precisely interpreting imaging data or even learning from past surgical experiences, thus improving surgical outcomes. The integration of machine learning not only empowers robots to perform specified functions with greater efficiency and accuracy but also enables them to learn from their operational experiences, constantly evolving and adapting to new challenges. As technology enthusiasts explore these innovations, they should consider the implications of machine learning in robotics not just from a technical standpoint but also from an ethical perspective. The evolution of intelligent robots raises questions about autonomy, decision-making processes, and the impact on human jobs. It is crucial to navigate these discussions thoughtfully, ensuring that advancements are leveraged for societal benefit. Embracing the ethos of responsible innovation helps assure that as robots become more intelligent, they enhance human capabilities rather than replace them. For those looking to delve deeper into this field, engaging with open-source machine learning frameworks can provide hands-on experience and understanding of how to develop and implement algorithms within robotic systems.

6.3 Tools and Frameworks for AI Robotics Programming

SEVERAL TOOLS AND FRAMEWORKS significantly enhance the process of developing AI for robotics, making complex concepts more accessible and actionable. Platforms such as Robot Operating System (ROS) have become essential, as they provide a vast library of robotics software and tools that streamline development. ROS facilitates communication between different parts of a robot, allowing developers to create modular code. This modularity ensures that components can be developed independently but also work seamlessly together, which is crucial for complex robotic systems. Frameworks like TensorFlow and PyTorch have also revolutionized the way AI algorithms can be implemented in robotic applications. They allow developers to build and train sophisticated machine learning models that can interpret sensory data and make decisions. The flexibility and scalability of these frameworks enable both beginners and advanced programmers to create innovative solutions tailored to specific challenges faced in robotics.

Open-source platforms play a vital role in the AI robotics community by fostering collaboration and innovation. They provide developers with access to a wealth of resources, including code libraries, tutorials, and community forums where ideas and solutions can be shared freely. This democratization of technology allows individuals and organizations with limited resources to contribute to advancements in robotics. Platforms such as OpenAI and GitHub have made it possible for anyone to experiment with cutting-edge AI models, pushing the boundaries of what robots can achieve. Open-source projects also encourage continuous improvement and adaptation, as contributions from various developers enhance the functionality and efficiency of existing tools. The sense of community around these platforms not only accelerates innovation but also nurtures a spirit of camaraderie among enthusiasts from all walks of life.

Using the right tools and embracing open-source collaboration can significantly impact the success of AI robotics projects. Developers looking to embark on a robotics journey should delve into the vast array of available frameworks and consider how they can leverage community resources to overcome challenges. Engaging in open-source projects not only enhances their skills but also contributes to a larger purpose, where their efforts can lead to meaningful advancements in how we interact with technology. Exploring existing repositories, participating in community discussions, and even contributing code can provide practical experience and insights, triggering the next wave of innovation in robotics and AI.

Chapter 7: Autonomous Navigation and Control

7.1 Techniques for Path Planning

PATH PLANNING FOR AUTONOMOUS navigation in robotics involves a range of algorithms designed to help robots understand and navigate their environments. One of the most popular algorithms is the A* (A-star) algorithm, which finds the shortest path from a start point to a goal by efficiently exploring the most promising paths first. Another widely used approach is Dijkstra's algorithm, which guarantees the shortest path but may be slower than A* since it explores all potential paths equally. For scenarios where real-time processing is crucial, Rapidly-exploring Random Trees (RRT) are favored. These algorithms work by random sampling in the space around the starting point and building a tree structure, rapidly connecting different areas and allowing for quick decision-making. Additionally, potential fields and Particle Swarm Optimization (PSO) are emerging techniques that facilitate path finding by treating obstacles as forces acting on the robot, steering it towards its goal while avoiding collisions.

Dynamic environments present unique challenges for path planning. Robots often have to react to moving obstacles, changing terrains, or new information that might arise. Traditional algorithms may struggle because they assume a static environment. To address this, dynamic path planning techniques such as the Dynamic Window Approach (DWA) come into play. This method considers both the robot's velocity and the movement of obstacles to calculate a safe path in real time. Another method involves using sensor fusion, which combines data from various sensors like LIDAR or cameras to create an updated model of the surroundings. Machine learning techniques are also increasingly being applied, enabling robots to predict and adapt to dynamic changes in their environment. These advancements help robots maintain their course and make intelligent adjustments on the fly, ensuring effective navigation even under unpredictable conditions.

Real-world applications of these algorithms are vast, ranging from self-driving cars that navigate busy streets to drone deliveries that find the most efficient flight paths. As technology continues to evolve, integrating these sophisticated path planning algorithms with artificial intelligence and deep learning promises even greater advancements in how robots interact with their environments. Understanding these techniques and their adaptability can provide insights for developers looking to implement robust navigation systems in their robotic projects. Balancing theoretical knowledge with practical experimentation will pave the way for breakthroughs in autonomous navigation.

7.2 Sensor Fusion for Navigation

SENSOR FUSION IS A critical technique that combines data from multiple sensors to enhance the accuracy and reliability of navigation systems. This concept draws from the understanding that no single sensor can provide a complete and unambiguous picture of the environment. By merging observations from different sources—such as GPS, inertial measurement units (IMUs), cameras, and LIDAR—a more precise and robust navigational solution can be achieved. This fusion of data helps to mitigate the shortcomings of individual sensors, such as the susceptibility to interference, noise, and errors, ultimately leading to improved navigational decisions in complex environments.

Various methods exist for merging sensor data effectively to create a coherent environmental model. One common approach is Kalman filtering, a mathematical method used to estimate the state of a dynamic system from a series of noisy measurements. This technique enables the prediction of the future state based on past data and helps to correct any inaccuracies in real-time. Another method is particle filtering, which utilizes a set of particles to represent the probability distribution of the state. This is particularly useful in non-linear and non-Gaussian environments, allowing for greater adaptability in diverse conditions. Additionally, machine learning techniques have emerged as powerful tools in sensor fusion, enabling systems to learn and improve their performance through experience, making them increasingly efficient at interpreting complex sensor data.

Incorporating sensor fusion in navigation systems requires not only technical prowess but also a philosophical approach to understanding how data interacts in the physical world. It's about recognizing that reality is often noisy and imperfect, yet with sophisticated merging techniques, it is possible to draw out clearer insights and guide actions with confidence. As technology continues to advance, staying informed about emerging sensor fusion methodologies and algorithms can dramatically enhance navigation applications, whether in autonomous vehicles, drones, or even wearable devices. Exploring sensor fusion techniques could lead to innovative advancements in precision navigation that push the boundaries of what we currently perceive as possible.

7.3 Control Algorithms for Autonomous Systems

VARIOUS CONTROL ALGORITHMS play a crucial role in enabling robot autonomy, allowing machines to operate independently in complex environments. One of the most common algorithms used is the Proportional-Integral-Derivative (PID) controller. This control strategy relies on feedback to make adjustments in real-time, ensuring that a robot can correct its course based on the difference between its current state and a predetermined goal. The PID algorithm combines three parameters: proportional control, which addresses the current error; integral control, which accumulates past errors; and derivative control, which anticipates future errors based on the rate of change. This blend creates a balanced response, making it suitable for various applications, from maintaining a steady speed to precise navigation.

Another powerful approach to control algorithms is reinforcement learning (RL). In this paradigm, an agent learns to make decisions through trial and error, receiving rewards or penalties based on its actions. Unlike traditional algorithms that rely heavily on predefined instructions, RL empowers robots to adapt to their surroundings by learning from experience. This adaptability is especially beneficial in dynamic environments where traditional PID controllers may struggle to deliver optimal performance. By simulating scenarios and allowing robots to explore, RL fosters a level of sophistication that elevates autonomous systems beyond simple, reactive behaviors.

The role of control algorithms in ensuring stable and reliable robot movement cannot be overstated. Stability is paramount; without it, robots risk oscillating uncontrollably or failing to complete tasks. Effective control algorithms allow robots to navigate obstacles smoothly, respond to unexpected changes, and maintain balance—essential qualities for versatile mobile platforms. Algorithms must not only focus on immediate corrections but also be designed to handle disturbances in the environment, ensuring that the robot maintains its trajectory and operational integrity. Selecting the right algorithm based on the specific application and environment greatly influences the system's overall efficiency and reliability. As we continue to develop autonomous systems, understanding and refining these control algorithms will be critical for achieving seamless, intelligent interactions between robots and their environments.

For those eager to delve into the world of robot autonomy, experimenting with PID tuning or engaging with reinforcement learning frameworks can provide invaluable hands-on experience. Practical implementation of these concepts can illuminate how subtle adjustments in algorithms might lead to significant improvements in performance, fostering ongoing innovation in the field.

Chapter 8: The Role of Data in AI Robotics

8.1 Data Collection Methods for Robotics

IDENTIFYING EFFECTIVE methods for data collection in robotics is crucial for the development and performance of robotic systems. Sensors play a fundamental role in this process, as they allow robots to gather real-time information about their environment. Various types of sensors, such as cameras, LIDAR, ultrasonic sensors, and IMUs (Inertial Measurement Units), each provide unique data that help robots perceive their surroundings. For instance, cameras can deliver essential visual data for object recognition and navigation, while LIDAR can create detailed three-dimensional maps of environments, crucial for autonomous navigation. Additionally, simulation tools like Gazebo and Webots serve as invaluable resources, enabling developers to simulate complex environments and scenarios without the physical limitations and hazards involved in real-world testing. These tools often incorporate physics engines that help replicate real-world interactions, allowing for extensive data collection that inform the design of more sophisticated algorithms and systems.

The significance of diverse data sets in training AI models for robotics cannot be overstated. A robust AI model relies on a rich repository of data that encompasses various scenarios, lighting conditions, and environmental factors. When robots are exposed to diverse data sets, they learn to generalize better and adapt to unforeseen conditions, making them more versatile and reliable in real-world applications. For example, a robot trained only on data from a specific type of terrain may struggle when deployed in a different environment, whereas one trained on varied terrains, including rocky, sandy, and uneven surfaces, can navigate them with greater ease. This diversity fosters resilience and adaptability, which are essential traits for advanced robotics. Moreover, collecting data that reflects different cultural contexts or user interactions can further enhance how robots engage with humans, making them more intuitive and effective in social settings.

In the quest to optimize robotic systems, combining sensor data and simulation results with a diverse range of training data is hugely beneficial. Engaging with different data collection methods, both in the physical and simulated environments, contributes to building more effective AI models. Consistently assessing and refining these models based on comprehensive and varied datasets accelerates the evolution of robotic technology, ultimately leading to smarter, more capable robots that can thrive in a multitude of settings.

8.2 Big Data Analytics in Robotics

BIG DATA ANALYTICS plays a pivotal role in enhancing the performance and decision-making processes of robotic systems. By harnessing vast streams of data generated from various sensors and interactions, robots can refine their operations, understand their environments better, and adapt to changes in real time. For instance, using machine learning algorithms, robots can analyze performance metrics and environmental parameters to optimize their tasks. This application allows them to learn from past experiences, enhancing their ability to perform complex functions autonomously. By integrating data analytics, robots can make informed decisions based on predictive modeling, leading to improved efficiency and accuracy in operations.

Several case studies illustrate the profound impact of data analysis in the field of robotics. One compelling example can be found in the agricultural sector, where robotic systems equipped with advanced sensors collect extensive data on soil health, crop conditions, and weather patterns. By processing this data, these robots can make real-time decisions about irrigation, pest control, and harvesting schedules, significantly increasing yield and reducing resource waste. Another noteworthy case study comes from the logistics industry, where companies like Amazon deploy fleets of autonomous robots. These robots utilize big data to optimize routing paths, manage inventory effectively, and even predict maintenance needs before failures occur, showcasing the critical role of data analytics in operational success.

In the context of evolving robotics, it becomes essential to recognize that the effective use of big data is not solely about collecting information. It's about transforming that data into actionable insights that can lead to smarter, faster, and more efficient robotic systems. Engaging in regular data analysis allows organizations to adapt and innovate, ensuring their robotic solutions meet the challenges of a fast-paced technological landscape. To further enhance robotic decision-making, exploring collaborative approaches in data sharing can drive innovation and accelerate advancements in robotics.

8.3 Data Privacy and Security in AI Robotics

DATA PRIVACY IN THE realm of AI robotics and autonomous systems faces significant challenges due to the vast amounts of information these technologies collect and process. Robots equipped with sensors and data-gathering capabilities often operate in personal or sensitive environments, such as homes or workplaces. This raises crucial concerns about how this data is collected, utilized, and stored. For instance, autonomous vehicles are constantly monitoring their surroundings, gathering data about passengers, the environment, and traffic conditions. If this data is not handled properly, it poses risks such as unauthorized access to personal information or misuse of sensitive data. Additionally, ensuring that this data is anonymized is essential, yet complex, as relationships between data points can sometimes reveal personal identities even after attempts to anonymize them. Organizations must navigate these complexities while maintaining compliance with legal frameworks like GDPR, which stress the importance of securing user consent and respecting individuals' rights to privacy.

To ensure data security while leveraging AI in robotics, best practices must be established and followed rigorously. Encryption plays a pivotal role in safeguarding data; it helps protect sensitive information from unauthorized access during transmission and storage. Additionally, implementing robust authentication mechanisms ensures that only authorized personnel can access the systems controlling these robots. Regular software updates are critical as well, patching vulnerabilities that could be exploited by malicious entities. The principle of least privilege should guide data access permissions, ensuring that individuals only have access to the data necessary for their work. Furthermore, organizational policies surrounding data handling and privacy should be clearly defined and communicated across all levels, so that everyone understands their responsibilities. When designing AI systems, embedding privacy by design principles fosters a culture of trust and security, as considerations for privacy are integrated into the development process from the beginning.

As technology enthusiasts explore the intersection of AI robotics and data privacy, staying informed about emerging technologies and practices that enhance data protection is essential. Consider engaging with community discussions on ethical AI use and privacy rights, and be proactive in advocating for transparency and accountability in how data is managed. One practical tip is to always scrutinize the privacy policies of any AI system or robotics technology you encounter. Understanding what data is collected, how it is used, and who it is shared with can empower you to make informed choices about your interactions with these systems. Remember, informed users are critical in shaping a future where data privacy and innovative tech coexist harmoniously.

Chapter 9: Human-Robot Interaction

9.1 Theories of Human-Robot Interaction

UNDERSTANDING HOW HUMANS and robots can effectively interact and communicate involves exploring key theories that illustrate the dynamics of this relationship. Social presence theory suggests that the degree to which a robot can appear socially engaging impacts how individuals perceive and interact with it. The more lifelike and responsive a robot seems, the more likely people will treat it as a social entity, fostering a connection that transcends mere utility. Similarly, the Uncanny Valley hypothesis proposes that as robots become more human-like, they elicit stronger emotional responses. However, if they appear too human-like without being convincingly lifelike, they may provoke discomfort or distaste. This phenomenon raises important questions about the ethical design of robots intended for social interaction, indicating that just a few subtle features can shift users' reactions from acceptance to aversion.

The implications of human-robot interaction on the design of robotic systems are profound. Designers must consider these psychological theories to create robots that enhance user experience while meeting functional requirements. For example, in healthcare settings, robots that assist with elderly care can be designed to be empathetic and user-friendly, ensuring that they communicate understanding through their actions and design. Responsiveness to human emotions, where robots can recognize and react appropriately to facial expressions or vocal tones, becomes vital in such contexts. Furthermore, incorporating natural language processing technologies enables robots to engage in fluid conversations, allowing for a more immersive interaction. It is essential for designers to strike a balance, integrating technological capabilities and psychological insights to enhance the usability and acceptance of robotic systems.

Focusing on these theories not only enriches the interplay between humans and robots but also supports the development of systems that are intuitive and responsive. When creating robots, designers can embed principles based on human psychology to facilitate smoother interactions, ultimately making technology more accessible and beneficial. Regular testing with human users helps refine these designs further, ensuring that they meet the needs and expectations of their environments. Keeping empathy and user experience at the forefront during the design process can make a significant difference in how well robots are received in various applications.

9.2 Designing User-Friendly Interfaces

USER-FRIENDLY INTERFACES are crucial in enhancing collaboration between humans and robots. These interfaces serve as the primary touchpoint for interaction, shaping how effectively humans can communicate their needs and commands to robotic systems. In an era where robotics increasingly integrates into everyday tasks, the clarity and intuitiveness of these interfaces can significantly impact user satisfaction and productivity. A well-designed interface minimizes cognitive load by allowing users to focus on their tasks rather than struggling with complex controls or unclear operations. When interfaces are intuitive, users can form a natural rapport with robots, fostering confidence in their collaborative abilities. This connection between design and user experience is vital, as it dictates not only how seamlessly a robot functions but also how readily users will accept and adapt to robotic assistance.

Several effective interface designs exemplify how intuitive interactions with robots can enhance usability. For instance, voice recognition systems that allow users to give verbal commands create a natural flow of communication. With technology like Amazon's Alexa or Google Assistant, users can interact with household robots simply and directly, transcending the need for complex programming or manual controls. Another example is the use of gesture-based controls in robotic systems, enabling users to manipulate robots through natural movements. This approach mirrors human communication and can lead to more fluid and instinctive interactions. Moreover, touch-screen interfaces that present clear and visually engaging information, such as the control panels on many modern industrial robots, help users make informed decisions quickly. Such designs capitalize on familiarity and combine visual cues with touch responsiveness, promoting a user-friendly experience.

As technology enthusiasts, understanding the principles behind these successful designs can inform your own efforts in creating or assessing user interfaces. Consider focusing on simplicity and clarity, ensuring that the most critical functions are easily accessible and that information is presented in a clear, digestible format. Emphasizing user feedback during the design process is also essential; real-world input can guide the refinement of your interface, ultimately leading to a more intuitive experience. Always remember that the goal of any interface is to enhance interaction rather than create barriers, allowing humans and robots to collaborate more effectively.

9.3 Social and Emotional Aspects of Interaction

THE DYNAMICS OF HUMAN-robot relationships are deeply influenced by psychological and emotional factors that govern human interactions. When people encounter robots, their responses are shaped by previous experiences, cultural backgrounds, and personal attitudes towards technology. For instance, trust plays a vital role, as individuals must feel safe and secure when interacting with robots, particularly in sensitive contexts such as healthcare or domestic environments. Emotional responses can also alter how humans perceive the competence and reliability of robots. A study showed that users tend to prefer robots that convey positive emotional feedback, such as smiles or encouraging gestures, as these cues foster a sense of connection. Understanding these factors is crucial for enhancing user experiences, as well-designed robots that elicit positive emotional reactions can lead to higher acceptance and engagement.

The role of social cues and emotional intelligence in robot design is pivotal for creating effective interactions. Social cues, such as eye contact, body language, and vocal tone, significantly influence how individuals relate to robots. For example, robots capable of mimicking human expressions or using naturalistic movements can create a sense of familiarity and comfort. Incorporating emotional intelligence into robots allows them to perceive and respond to human emotions, increasing their utility in various applications. This emotional responsiveness can be implemented through advanced algorithms that interpret voice tone or facial expressions, enabling robots to adjust their behavior accordingly. In design, incorporating these emotional and social cues not only improves user satisfaction but also enhances the functionality and effectiveness of robots in social settings.

In an age where technology increasingly becomes part of our everyday lives, fostering meaningful human-robot interactions is essential. Designers and engineers should prioritize understanding the emotional needs of users and integrate this understanding into the development of robots. This approach will ultimately lead to machines that not only serve practical purposes but also enrich human experience by being responsive and relatable. Experiment with various design elements that resonate emotionally and observe how they influence user interactions; what connects us often goes beyond functionality.

Chapter 10: Robotics in Various Industries

10.1 AI Robotics in Healthcare

THE REVOLUTIONARY IMPACT of AI robotics in healthcare is transforming the way medical professionals deliver patient care and make diagnostic decisions. These technologies, powered by sophisticated algorithms and machine learning, enable a level of precision and efficiency that was previously unattainable. For instance, AI systems can analyze vast amounts of medical data with remarkable speed, helping healthcare providers identify patterns and potential issues that might go unnoticed in traditional examination methods. This enhancement leads to earlier diagnoses and more tailored treatment plans, ultimately resulting in better patient outcomes.

Moreover, the use of robotics in surgical settings has brought new dimensions to the operating room. Robots assist surgeons by providing enhanced visualization and dexterity, making complex procedures less invasive and reducing recovery times for patients. Technologies like robotic arms equipped with AI can perform intricate tasks with precision that minimizes human error. This collaborative approach between human skill and robotic assistance not only increases the safety of surgeries but also allows for innovations such as remote surgeries, where specialists can operate on patients from different geographic locations. Rehabilitation is another area where robots play a critical role. Robotic exoskeletons and personalized rehabilitation devices aid in the recovery process, allowing patients to regain mobility and strength with guided support. These transformational technologies bridge the gap between human ability and mechanical support, promoting a faster return to normal life activities.

As the integration of AI and robotics advances, ethical considerations also emerge, challenging us to ponder the balance between technology and human touch in healthcare. While these innovations enhance efficiency and outcomes, it is essential to maintain the compassionate element inherent to medical practice. The future of healthcare must focus not only on the marvels of technology but also on the preservation of the human connection between caregivers and patients. Knowing how to navigate this landscape will be vital for healthcare professionals and tech enthusiasts alike. Exploring further into this intersection, one might consider how continuous education and open dialogues about the implications of AI in healthcare can foster an environment where technology is harnessed responsibly and effectively, ensuring comprehensive care for all.

10.2 Automation in Manufacturing and Logistics

THE INTEGRATION OF AI robotics into manufacturing and logistics plays a crucial role in transforming traditional processes, boosting productivity across diverse industries. AI-powered robots are designed to handle repetitive and labor-intensive tasks, allowing human workers to focus on more complex and creative activities. These robots enhance efficiency by operating with high precision, reducing human error and increasing the speed of manufacturing and logistics processes. The result is a streamlined workflow, where materials and products move seamlessly from one stage to the next, significantly minimizing downtime and bottlenecks that once plagued the industry.

Innovations such as warehouse robots stand out as game-changers in this landscape. These autonomous machines are capable of navigating vast storage facilities, locating items, and transporting goods with remarkable agility. Equipped with advanced sensors and AI algorithms, warehouse robots can adapt to dynamic environments, maximizing storage space while ensuring quick retrieval and delivery of products. This not only accelerates order fulfillment but also optimizes the overall supply chain, making it more resilient to fluctuations in demand and minimizing operational costs. As warehouses become increasingly automated, the demand for skilled labor shifts towards roles that require critical thinking, problem-solving, and advanced technical knowledge.

Understanding the implications of this technological shift is essential for those invested in the future of manufacturing and logistics. Emphasizing the importance of continuous learning and adaptation can empower individuals and organizations to thrive in an increasingly automated world. Staying updated on advancements in AI and robotics can enable businesses to leverage new tools effectively, creating opportunities for growth and innovation. Exploring hands-on experiences with emerging technologies can foster a deep appreciation for their potential, as well as critical insights into how these innovations can be harnessed for a competitive advantage.

10.3 Robotics in Agriculture and Environmental Management

ARTIFICIAL INTELLIGENCE (AI) robotics is playing a transformative role in agriculture, particularly through the concepts of precision farming and automation. Precision farming involves using GPS technology, sensors, and drones to monitor crop conditions and soil health. This level of detail allows farmers to make informed decisions about when to plant, irrigate, and harvest their crops. AI-enabled robots can analyze vast amounts of data, helping farmers understand the specific needs of their fields. For instance, some robots can detect variations in soil moisture levels and automatically adjust irrigation systems accordingly. This not only optimizes water usage but also enhances crop yield by ensuring that each plant receives the exact resources it requires. Furthermore, autonomous tractors equipped with AI can perform tasks such as plowing and planting with minimal human intervention, significantly reducing labor costs and increasing efficiency.

In addition to revolutionizing agriculture, robotics also has significant applications in environmental management. Robots and drones equipped with sensors are increasingly used for monitoring ecosystems, tracking wildlife, and assessing the health of forests and oceans. For example, drones can collect data on deforestation rates or monitor wildlife populations from the air, offering insights that are difficult to obtain through traditional methods. Moreover, robotics plays a crucial role in conservation efforts. Robots designed to clean oceans can collect plastic waste and other pollutants, contributing to the restoration of marine environments. Such applications not only highlight the potential of these technologies in protecting our planet but also encourage a more sustainable approach to environmental management. By integrating robotics into various environmental initiatives, we can gather data more efficiently, helping conservationists plan better strategies to preserve biodiversity.

The intersection of robotics, agriculture, and environmental management offers a multitude of possibilities. For those invested in technology and environmental sustainability, staying informed about advancements in robotic systems can foster new ideas and innovations. Engaging with local agricultural programs or environmental organizations that utilize robotics can provide hands-on experience and insights into how these technologies are shaping the future.

Chapter 11: Emerging Technologies in AI Robotics

11.1 Soft Robotics and Its Applications

SOFT ROBOTICS IS AN exciting and rapidly evolving field that redefines traditional engineering principles by incorporating materials and designs that mimic biological organisms. Unlike conventional robots, which are often rigid and limited by mechanical constraints, soft robots are made from pliable materials such as silicone, hydrogels, and elastomers. This flexibility allows them to adapt to complex environments and interact safely with surrounding objects and humans. The innovative approaches in soft robotics challenge the norms of design, focusing on responsive structures that can perform tasks that were once thought impossible for machines. By utilizing actuation methods inspired by nature, such as pneumatic or hydraulic systems, soft robots can perform delicate movements, making them ideal candidates for a variety of applications.

Soft robots find their niche in numerous fields where safety and adaptability are critical. In the medical domain, such robots can assist during surgeries by providing delicate manipulations without causing harm to tissues. They serve as assistive devices for rehabilitating patients, helping them regain mobility while ensuring comfort during the recovery process. In agriculture, soft robots are engineered to handle fragile crops with care, reducing damage and increasing yield. Additionally, their capabilities extend to the realm of search and rescue operations, where soft robots can navigate through rubble or uneven terrain, helping to locate trapped individuals. The ability to safely interact with humans makes soft robots promising tools in personal care and companionship roles, particularly for the elderly or disabled.

The philosophical implications of soft robotics also provoke thought; they challenge our fundamental understanding of intelligence and consciousness. As we design robots that can adapt and learn from their environments, we must ponder the boundaries between biological and artificial life forms. This fusion of engineering and living principles prompts us to rethink our relationship with technology, as soft robots integrate into our daily lives, improving safety and efficiency. These advancements open exciting avenues for exploration in materials science and robotics, paving the way for countless future innovations. Staying updated on the latest research and developments in soft robotics can provide technology enthusiasts with insights into potential career paths and educational opportunities in this groundbreaking field.

11.2 Collaborative Robots (Cobots)

COLLABORATIVE ROBOTS, commonly referred to as cobots, are innovative machines designed to work alongside human operators in a shared workspace. Unlike traditional industrial robots that are often confined to cages or separated from human interaction for safety reasons, cobots are built with advanced safety features, including sensors and intelligent programming, allowing them to perform tasks in close proximity to people. This integration of cobots in human work environments signifies a shift in how automation is approached. These robots can assist in various tasks such as assembly, material handling, and quality control without the need for stringent safety barriers, thus enabling a fluid and efficient workflow that enhances human capabilities rather than replaces them.

Numerous industries are witnessing the benefits of incorporating cobots into their operations. For instance, in manufacturing settings, companies like BMW have harnessed the power of collaborative robots on their assembly lines. These cobots assist workers by lifting heavy components or performing repetitive tasks, which not only increases productivity but also reduces the physical strain on human employees. Another compelling example is found in the healthcare sector, where cobots are being used to assist in surgeries or to transport materials within hospitals, minimizing the risk of cross-contamination and improving overall safety. By sharing duties with humans, cobots not only enhance productivity but also help create a safer work environment. They are particularly useful in environments where precision and consistency are essential, supporting teams in achieving higher accuracy and repeatability in tasks.

To maximize the potential of cobots, organizations should focus on continuous training and upskilling for their workforce. This ensures that employees are well-acquainted with the technology and can collaborate effectively with robotic systems. Implementing cobots is not just about technology; it's about fostering a culture of cooperation between humans and machines. By encouraging this partnership, companies can not only improve efficiency but also drive innovation across their operations. The future of work will likely see cobots taking on more complex tasks, underscoring the importance of adaptability and an open mindset toward learning new technologies.

11.3 Drones and Autonomous Vehicles

THE ADVANCEMENTS IN drones and autonomous vehicles have marked a significant leap in technological innovation. These machines, once relegated to the realm of science fiction, are now integral to our daily lives and industries. Drones have evolved from mere remote-controlled gadgets into sophisticated systems capable of performing complex tasks autonomously. Similarly, autonomous vehicles have transitioned from early prototypes to vehicles that can navigate, understand, and interact with their environment. The groundbreaking technologies enabling these innovations include artificial intelligence, machine learning, and advanced sensor systems, allowing for improved decision-making and safety. With growing interest in their potential, both industries witness rapid development and investment shaping future possibilities.

The applications of drones and autonomous vehicles span an impressive range of sectors, fundamentally changing how we approach tasks and solve problems. In logistics, drones are employed for swift delivery of goods, especially in hard-to-reach areas, while companies like Amazon experiment with delivering packages directly to customers' doorsteps via drone fleets. In agriculture, drones help monitor crop health, offering farmers real-time data to enhance productivity without relying solely on traditional methods. On the other hand, autonomous vehicles are gaining traction in public transport, with self-driving shuttles gradually being introduced in urban environments. Moreover, they play an essential role in surveillance and security, providing law enforcement with aerial perspectives that aid in monitoring large areas effectively. This technological evolution raises philosophical questions surrounding trust, privacy, and the ethical implications of automating decision-making processes in our society.

The implications of these innovations extend beyond efficiency and convenience. As both drone and autonomous vehicle technologies continue to develop, they promise broader accessibility and sustainable practices, reshaping urban landscapes and logistics networks. However, as we embrace this future, it is vital to remain mindful of the challenges, such as regulatory hurdles, safety concerns, and the impact on employment sectors. Staying informed about these advancements and advocating for thoughtful integration into society can help ensure that these technologies serve humanity positively and equitably. Understanding the potential and limitations of drones and autonomous vehicles empowers technology enthusiasts to engage with these developments critically and creatively, remaining at the forefront of this transformative era.

Chapter 12: The Future of AI Robotics

12.1 Trends Shaping the Future

CURRENT TRENDS IN AI robotics reveal a dynamic landscape transforming industries and everyday life. Increased integration of machine learning algorithms allows robots to learn from their environment and improve their performance over time. This capability is evident in autonomous vehicles, where AI systems process vast amounts of data to make real-time driving decisions. Collaborative robots, or cobots, are also gaining traction in manufacturing settings. By working alongside human operators, they enhance productivity while ensuring safety in shared workspaces. Furthermore, advancements in natural language processing enable robots to communicate more effectively, building a more intuitive human-robot interaction framework. These trends indicate that the robotics industry is heading towards a future where adaptability and collaboration are at the core of its development, fundamentally altering our approach to work and life.

Potential technological breakthroughs on the horizon could redefine robotics in unprecedented ways. One such breakthrough is the development of soft robotics, which utilizes flexible materials to create robots that can safely interact with delicate objects and navigate complex environments. This could be revolutionary in fields such as healthcare, where robots assist in surgeries or patient care without risking harm. Another promising area is the enhancement of energy efficiency through advanced power sources, including bio-inspired batteries or wireless charging technologies, allowing robots to operate longer without the need for frequent recharging. Additionally, breakthroughs in AI could lead to the creation of self-aware robots that possess the ability to make ethical decisions, raising profound philosophical questions about autonomy and responsibility. As these advancements unfold, we may witness a shift in how society perceives and integrates robots into daily life, prompting a deeper dialogue about the role of technology in our future.

Staying informed about these trends and breakthroughs is essential for technology enthusiasts. The evolving landscape of AI robotics not only presents opportunities for innovation but also challenges us to consider the implications of these technologies. Engaging with forums, attending conferences, and following thought leaders in the field can provide valuable insights and enhance your understanding of where robotics is headed. Keeping an open mind and being adaptable will empower you to navigate and contribute to this exciting future.

12.2 The Role of AI Robotics in Society

THE INTEGRATION OF AI robotics into daily life carries profound societal implications. In recent years, we have seen robots doing everything from mundane household chores to complex surgical procedures. Their presence is increasing in sectors like manufacturing, healthcare, transportation, and even entertainment. This raises critical questions about the future of human labor, as these machines can often perform tasks with greater efficiency and accuracy. While the efficiency gains may lead to economic growth, there is also mounting concern regarding job displacement and the potential widening of social inequalities. As robots become more capable, society must consider how to adapt to these changes, ensuring that the benefits of AI technology are shared broadly rather than falling into the hands of a privileged few. Furthermore, the emotional and psychological ramifications of daily interactions with robots cannot be overlooked; as we integrate these machines into our routines, we begin to modify our expectations for human interaction and connection.

Balancing technological advancement with ethical considerations is crucial in this evolving landscape. As AI systems become more autonomous and intelligent, we are faced with dilemmas revolving around accountability, decision-making, and privacy. For instance, if an autonomous vehicle causes an accident, who is responsible? The developer, the manufacturer, or the owner? These questions underline the necessity of creating guidelines and regulations that prioritize ethical standards. Additionally, as robots become more integrated into personal lives, issues of data privacy arise; they often collect vast amounts of information to learn and improve. Establishing a trust framework that assures users their data will be handled ethically and securely is essential for fostering acceptance and reliance on these technologies. Striking a balance between innovation and ethical safeguard demands continuous dialogue among technologists, ethicists, lawmakers, and society at large. It is not simply a question of what we can do, but what we should do.

As we navigate this rapidly changing environment, it is beneficial for technology enthusiasts to engage with the ethical discourse surrounding AI robotics. By understanding the implications of these technologies and advocating for responsible practices, individuals can play a crucial role in shaping a future where both innovation and humanity thrive. Embracing education and dialogue will help us responsibly integrate AI and robotics into our lives, ultimately leading to a society where technology enhances our human experience rather than detracting from it. Keeping abreast of developments in this field, staying informed about ethical considerations, and fostering discussions in your communities can make a significant difference in how we collectively manage the transition into a more automated world.

12.3 Speculations: AI Robotics in the Next Decade

OVER THE NEXT DECADE, AI robotics is poised to undergo significant developments driven by advancements in machine learning, sensor technology, and ethical considerations. One can envision robots becoming more adept at processing vast amounts of data in real time, allowing them to make more autonomous decisions. However, this potential is coupled with challenges such as ensuring safety, security, and the ethical implications of machines operating independently within society. As robots become more integrated into daily life, questions surrounding accountability will become paramount. Who is responsible when a robot malfunctions or causes harm? Additionally, the workforce will experience monumental changes as AI robots take on roles traditionally held by humans, from manufacturing to healthcare, raising concerns about job displacement and socioeconomic disparities. The ability to adapt to these changes will be crucial for individuals and organizations alike, as they navigate a landscape where human and robotic collaboration becomes the norm.

The integration of AI robotics into future societal frameworks could reshape how we interact, work, and live. We might see robots assisting in homes, providing companionship for the elderly, or delivering essential services in urban areas. Educational environments could be transformed with personal learning assistants capable of tailoring their teaching strategies to individual student needs. A more harmonious coexistence between humans and robots hinges on societal acceptance and ethical frameworks that guide AI development. For successful integration, robust policies must be established to regulate the use of robotics technologies while promoting transparency in AI algorithms. Public engagement and education will play vital roles in fostering a culture that embraces innovation while prioritizing ethical standards over sheer technological capability.

As we speculate about the future of AI robotics, it is essential to focus on the balance between advancement and ethics. Continuous dialogue among technologists, policymakers, and the public will be necessary to ensure that the benefits of AI robotics are equitably distributed. Addressing challenges and optimizing integration will unlock new possibilities for enhancing human potential through technology. One practical tip for anyone interested in this field is to stay informed by following reputable sources in AI and robotics. Engaging in discussions and participating in community forums can offer valuable perspectives that reflect the evolving intersection of humanity and technology.

Chapter 13: DIY AI Robotics Projects

13.1 Getting Started with Basic Projects

EMBARKING ON YOUR FIRST DIY robotics project can feel daunting, yet it is a journey fueled by curiosity and creativity. A clear roadmap can guide you through this exciting path, starting with understanding the fundamentals of robotics. Begin with a simple concept: what do you want your robot to do? Defining a clear goal will frame your project and make subsequent decisions easier. Next, familiarize yourself with basic programming knowledge, as this will be crucial regardless of the robotics you choose to pursue. Many newcomers benefit from existing tutorials and community forums, where ideas and support flow freely. This collaboration can spark inspiration for your first project.

Equipping yourself with the essential tools and components is a crucial step in turning your ideas into reality. A basic robotics toolkit should include a soldering iron, small hand tools like screwdrivers, and a multimeter for troubleshooting your circuits. As for components, start with a microcontroller, such as an Arduino or Raspberry Pi, which serve as the brain of your robot. Include motors for movement, sensors to interact with the environment, and wheels or tracks for mobility. Don't underestimate the role of a sturdy chassis; it can be made from readily available materials, like plastic or wood. These building blocks provide a strong foundation from which you can expand your projects and explore more complex designs.

One practical tip to remember is to keep your projects modular. It allows you to upgrade parts or modify functions without starting from scratch each time. This approach not only saves time but also enhances learning. Each project you complete will empower you with skills and knowledge for the next, making your journey through the world of robotics not just productive, but profoundly rewarding.

13.2 Intermediate Robotics Projects with AI

AS THE FIELD OF ROBOTICS continues to evolve, DIY enthusiasts are increasingly drawn to more sophisticated projects that incorporate elements of artificial intelligence. This chapter delves into advanced robotics projects that not only challenge your technical abilities but also expand your understanding of how AI can enhance robotic functionality. These projects require a combination of programming skills, mechanical knowledge, and an understanding of AI concepts, pushing you to synthesize these domains into cohesive systems. By engaging in such undertakings, you develop not just practical skills, but also a philosophical appreciation for the intersection of technology and human creativity. Imagine constructing a robot designed to navigate complex environments using advanced computer vision and machine learning algorithms. Such projects are not merely about assembling parts but involve a deep dive into the programmable nature of intelligence itself, prompting you to consider how machines can learn from their surroundings and experiences.

Project ideas that apply practical AI concepts in robotics offer exciting pathways for innovation. Consider creating a self-driving vehicle prototype using a Raspberry Pi or Arduino, with the addition of AI capabilities like obstacle recognition and route optimization. This project could involve implementing neural networks that analyze sensor data to make real-time decisions, effectively showcasing how AI algorithms can improve navigation and safety. Alternatively, you might explore building a robotic arm that employs reinforcement learning to master tasks like sorting objects based on their characteristics. This experience can illuminate the application of AI in enhancing precision and efficiency in robotic operations. Each of these projects demands a step beyond basic programming and into the realm of designing systems that mimic cognitive functions. You'll find yourself challenged not only to troubleshoot technical issues but also to think critically about the implications of autonomous decision-making and machine learning.

While exploring these advanced robotics projects, it's essential to keep in mind that the learning curve may be steep, but the rewards are substantial. Engaging with AI-enabled robotics not only hones your technical skills but also deepens your understanding of emerging technologies that are increasingly relevant in our world. As you work through these projects, consider documenting your journey, sharing insights and challenges with fellow enthusiasts. This not only reinforces your learning but contributes to the collective knowledge within the robotics community. Remember, the most successful projects often result from iterative improvement and collaboration, encouraging you to experiment, adapt, and refine your designs. Take the time to reflect on how your work fits into the larger picture of technological progress, as this perspective can inspire further creativity and innovation in your future endeavors.

13.3 Resources for DIY Robotics Enthusiasts

FOR THOSE DIVING INTO the world of DIY robotics, a plethora of resources is available online that can significantly enhance your learning experience. Websites such as Instructables, Make: Magazine, and Adafruit are treasure troves of tutorials spanning from beginner projects to advanced builds, often accompanied by step-by-step instructions and community insights. Online forums like Reddit's r/robotics and the DIY

Drones community provide platforms for enthusiasts to ask questions, share progress, and troubleshoot problems together. These spaces encourage collaboration and creativity, nurturing a vibrant atmosphere where both novice and expert builders come together. Additionally, platforms such as GitHub host numerous open-source robotics projects, offering the opportunity to study existing code, contribute to projects, or even start your own. YouTube is another invaluable resource, with channels dedicated to robotics that offer visual guidance and practical demonstrations, greatly aiding those who learn best through observation. Furthermore, websites such as Coursera and edX provide courses in robotics and related fields, enabling individuals to grasp theoretical underpinnings that support hands-on efforts.

Finding support and inspiration within the DIY robotics community can transform your experience from a solitary endeavor into a communal journey. Engaging with local maker spaces or robotics clubs can provide real-world connections with like-minded individuals who share your passion. These communities often host workshops, competitions, and collaborative projects that create an engaging environment for hands-on learning and experimentation. Online platforms, such as Discord servers and Facebook groups focused on robotics, also play a crucial role in sustaining engagement and encouraging newcomers. Networking within these groups allows you to exchange ideas, receive constructive feedback, and gain exposure to diverse perspectives and skills that can enhance your projects. Attending robotics competitions or expos can also serve as powerful motivators, where witnessing innovative designs, demos, and presentations sparks new ideas and encourages you to push the boundaries of your own creativity. Connecting with mentors within these communities can further propel your journey, providing a guiding hand that enriches both technical skills and strategic thinking.

Ultimately, the DIY robotics community thrives on a spirit of sharing and collaboration. It's not just about acquiring knowledge but also about fostering relationships that can lead to innovative solutions and breakthroughs. A practical tip is to document your progress and share it within these communities. Whether you choose to blog, post videos, or simply participate in discussions, sharing your journey can not only inspire others but also attract valuable feedback that enriches your learning experience.

Chapter 14: Philosophical Implications of AI Robotics

14.1 The Nature of Consciousness and Robotics

PHILOSOPHERS HAVE LONG debated the essence of consciousness, pondering whether it is a uniquely human trait or something that can be replicated. In the context of artificial intelligence and robotics, these questions take on a new urgency as we progress toward creating machines that exhibit behaviors akin to human thought and awareness. The philosophical conundrum of whether machines could ever possess true consciousness persists. If robots can analyze data, learn from their environment, and even make decisions based on complex algorithms, do they not approach a form of consciousness? Observing and responding to stimuli in a way that resembles human interaction could lead us to recognize artificial agents as entities that participate in some form of experiential awareness, often referred to as machine consciousness. However, whether this awareness amounts to genuine consciousness or merely mimics human behavior remains a contested philosophical point.

The implications of developing robots with advanced cognitive abilities extend into every facet of society, raising ethical, social, and technological questions. For instance, if robots were to achieve a level of cognitive complexity that allows for emotional responses or ethical decision-making, we would need to reconsider our legal and moral frameworks. Should these robots have rights, or are they simply tools designed to enhance human capability? Moreover, the potential for robots to engage in social interactions and relationships with humans transforms our understanding of companionship and support, particularly in sectors like healthcare and eldercare. The prospect of creating empathetic robots opens doors to significant innovations but also invites caution. We must grapple with concerns over dependency on these machines and the consequences of integrating sentient-like beings into daily life.

As technology enthusiasts exploring the intersection of consciousness and robotics, it's vital to engage with these philosophical discussions. Understanding the ramifications of our advancements helps navigate the ethical mazes ahead. For those involved in designing and programming AI systems, awareness of these issues can guide responsible innovation. Recognizing that the development of sophisticated cognitive abilities in robots is more than a technical challenge; it demands an alignment of moral values, societal impact, and an unwavering commitment to ensuring that the journey into artificial consciousness benefits humanity as a whole.

14.2 Ethical Dilemmas in AI Robotics

THE DEVELOPMENT AND use of AI robotics raise numerous ethical challenges that society must navigate carefully. As robots become more autonomous and capable of making decisions, questions surface about the moral implications of their actions. For instance, when a robot is programmed to assist in surgery or drive a car, its decisions can have life-altering consequences. The potential for error or malicious programming challenges creators and users to consider the ramifications of technology. Issues such as bias in algorithms, privacy concerns, and the safety of human interactions with machines highlight the delicate balance required. Ethical dilemmas also emerge in military applications where robots may be tasked with making decisions in warfare, leading to concerns about accountability for actions taken in conflict zones.

The moral responsibility of creators and companies in deploying robotics technologies cannot be overstated. Developers must recognize that with great power comes great responsibility. They are, in essence, setting the frameworks within which these machines operate, and thus their ethical considerations should extend throughout the entire lifecycle of the technology. This includes ensuring that robots are designed to maximize benefits while minimizing harm. Companies must engage in transparent practices, hold themselves accountable for outcomes, and prioritize the ethical implications of their technological advancements over sheer profit. As robotics integrate further into everyday life, the groundwork for responsible AI development will define not only the future of technology but also the moral fabric of society.

To navigate these ethical landscapes, ongoing dialogue among technologists, ethicists, policymakers, and the public is crucial. Understanding the implications of AI robotics is essential in fostering a future where technology serves humanity without compromising ethical integrity. It is beneficial for companies involved in robotics to adopt rigorous ethical reviews and to involve diverse perspectives in their development processes. This approach not only addresses potential dilemmas before they arise but also contributes to a more thoughtful and inclusive technological advancement.

14.3 AI Robotics and the Human Experience

AI ROBOTICS HAS THE potential to significantly redefine our perceptions of companionship, work, and human relationships. Traditionally, companionship has been rooted in human connections, marked by emotional responses, shared experiences, and mutual understanding. However, as we integrate AI-driven robots into our lives, the boundary between human and artificial companionship begins to blur. AI companions can perform tasks, engage in conversation, and even learn from their interactions, creating a semblance of relationship dynamics that many find comforting or fulfilling. For individuals who may experience loneliness, these AI companions could provide a form of support that is both accessible and reliable, fostering companionship where it may have otherwise been lacking. In workplaces, the introduction of AI robotics is shifting the labor landscape. Tasks that were once solely performed by humans are now being delegated to robots, raising questions about job displacement and the evolution of work itself. Far from replacing humans entirely, AI robotics can serve as augmentation tools, allowing workers to focus on more complex, creative tasks while robots handle repetitive or outright dangerous activities. This transformation has profound implications for how we perceive our professional identities and the nature of collaboration between humans and machines.

The enrichment of the human experience through AI robotics presents both opportunities and challenges. On one hand, these technologies can enhance our capabilities, offering solutions that improve our daily lives, from personalized healthcare to smart home management. The ability to program AI to learn about individual preferences enriches our experience, making interactions more meaningful and customized. This level of personalization can lead to greater productivity and satisfaction, particularly in environments that adapt to the needs of their users. However, the incorporation of AI robotics also complicates human experiences. Relying too heavily on robotic systems might lead to diminished interpersonal skills as we grow accustomed to engaging with machines rather than people. The emotional nuances that come with human interaction could be lost in translation when mediated by AI. Furthermore, ethical considerations arise; how do we ensure that AI behaves in ways that are aligned with human values? As we embrace this technology, it's vital to maintain a balance that prioritizes genuine human interaction alongside the efficiencies that AI robotics can provide.

Understanding the dual-edged nature of AI in our lives is crucial as technology enthusiasts. Recognizing that while AI robotics can enrich our companionship, work, and relationships, they can also introduce layers of complexity calls for mindful engagement with this technology. Remain curious, question the evolving norms of your interactions, and foster connections that enhance rather than replace the irreplaceable qualities of human relationships. Embracing AI robotics doesn't mean abandoning our humanity; it means integrating new tools into our lives while preserving what makes human connection unique.

Chapter 15: Community and Collaboration in AI Robotics

15.1 Fostering Innovation through Community Projects

COMMUNITY-DRIVEN PROJECTS play a pivotal role in advancing innovation in AI robotics. They stand as a testament to the power of collective effort, where individuals from diverse backgrounds unite to solve common problems. These projects often harness local expertise and creativity, leading to innovative solutions that might not emerge in more conventional corporate or academic environments. When communities come together, they foster an atmosphere of collaboration that is vital for experimentation and risk-taking, which are essential components of innovation. In the realm of AI robotics, this collaboration can lead to the creation of new algorithms, hardware integrations, and applications that are grounded in real-world needs. Moreover, by engaging people from various disciplines — engineers, artists, educators, and even policy-makers — community projects ensure that multiple perspectives shape the technological landscape. This multidimensional approach not only increases the relevance of AI solutions but also enhances their adaptability, ensuring they can be effectively integrated into everyday life.

Examining successful collaborative projects reveals how community initiatives have made significant impacts in the field of AI robotics. One notable example is the open-source robotics initiative, ROS (Robot

Operating System), which has seen collaborative contributions from engineers and researchers globally. By allowing users to share code and ideas freely, ROS has accelerated the development of robotics applications, enabling organizations both large and small to innovate without the burden of extensive financial investment. Another inspiring project is MIT's Media Lab, where interdisciplinary teams work on various projects that merge technology with social good. Their initiatives focus on designing robots that assist in education, healthcare, and even disaster relief, showcasing how community engagement can produce robots that are not only advanced but also socially responsible. These initiatives highlight the profound impact of collaboration and demonstrate that innovation does not solely reside within the confines of established tech companies, but flourishes in the diverse ideas and talents that community projects cultivate.

With the surge of interest in AI robotics, technology enthusiasts can benefit from exploring and participating in local community projects. Engaging with these initiatives not only amplifies individual learning but also contributes to the broader ecosystem of innovation. By collaborating with others, sharing knowledge, and tackling real-world challenges together, enthusiasts can gain hands-on experience that is invaluable in today's fast-evolving tech landscape. Encouraging involvement in community projects can also lead to unexpected partnerships and ideas, which are often the catalysts for breakthrough innovations. As technology continues to evolve, actively participating in and fostering community-driven initiatives will ensure that the field remains dynamic, inclusive, and responsive to the needs of society.

15.2 Online Platforms for Collaboration

NUMEROUS ONLINE PLATFORMS have emerged as vital hubs for AI robotics enthusiasts and professionals seeking collaboration. Websites such as GitHub serve as repositories for open-source projects, allowing users to share their coding advancements and contribute to collective projects. Forums like Reddit host specialized communities where individuals can pose questions, share breakthroughs, or discuss challenges they face in their robotics endeavors. Platforms like Discord and Slack have also gained traction, facilitating real-time communication among groups working on similar projects. These platforms enable accessibility for users at all levels, from novices to seasoned experts, thereby creating an inclusive environment where ideas flourish.

These online platforms act as catalysts for networking and knowledge-sharing opportunities. By connecting users from diverse backgrounds, they promote a wealth of perspectives that enrich discussions and drive innovation. For instance, professionals might share insights from their industry experience, while hobbyists bring fresh, unconventional approaches to problem-solving. By engaging in discussions, contributing to projects, or attending webinars hosted on these platforms, users can cultivate valuable relationships that often lead to collaborative ventures. The exchange of knowledge in these spaces not only enhances individual understanding but can also ignite new projects, encouraging a culture of continuous learning and development.

In the realm of AI robotics, staying updated with the latest advancements is crucial. Therefore, actively participating in these online platforms can provide significant advantages. Users should consider regular engagement—taking part in discussions, sharing findings, or even organizing virtual meetups. These actions not only expand one's circle but also contribute to the broader community, fostering a collaborative spirit that empowers collective growth.

15.3 Networking Opportunities for AI Robotics Creators

ATTENDING CONFERENCES, workshops, and meetups in the AI robotics community is an invaluable experience that can profoundly impact your career and projects. These events serve as platforms for exchanging ideas, knowledge, and innovations. When you immerse yourself in a gathering of like-minded tech enthusiasts, you open the door to insights that are often not accessible through textbooks or online courses. The hands-on opportunities at these events allow you to engage directly with experts in the field, providing you with unique perspectives on emerging trends, challenges, and solutions in AI and robotics. Furthermore, interactions with peers can spark new ideas and ignite creativity, enriching your understanding of your own work. By attending these forums, you not only expand your technical prowess but also develop a sense of community that is essential in a field characterized by rapid evolution and continuous collaboration.

Exploring potential partnerships and synergies that arise from networking can lead to extraordinary advancements in your projects. When creators come together, they can synergize their skills and resources to tackle complex problems more effectively. For instance, an AI developer might find a robotics engineer whose hardware expertise complements their software innovations, leading to the development of smarter, more efficient systems. These connections can evolve into formal collaborations where shared goals combine with individual strengths, creating solutions that neither could achieve alone. Additionally, networking can facilitate introductions to investors and industry leaders who can provide vital support, both financially and strategically. This kind of cooperative spirit nurtures an ecosystem where innovation flourishes and progressive thinking becomes the norm, ultimately enhancing the impact of AI robotics on society.

Engage proactively with others in the field. Make a habit of sharing what you learn and your experiences, as this openness not only helps others but also solidifies your reputation within the community. When you actively participate, whether through Q&A sessions, presenting at workshops, or simply engaging in discussions, you establish yourself as a valuable member of the network. Building relationships is crucial; follow up with contacts after events and maintain those connections through social media or professional platforms like LinkedIn. Taking these steps ensures a continuous flow of inspiration and knowledge, keeping you at the forefront of technological advancements in AI and robotics.

Don't miss out!

Visit the website below and you can sign up to receive emails whenever M.S. Ali publishes a new book. There's no charge and no obligation.

https://books2read.com/r/B-A-LCWBD-TMTEG

BOOKS 2 READ

Connecting independent readers to independent writers.

Did you love *Mind in Motion: AI Robotics for the Curious Creator*? Then you should read *AI and the Future: The Algorithmic Age*[1] by M.S. Ali!

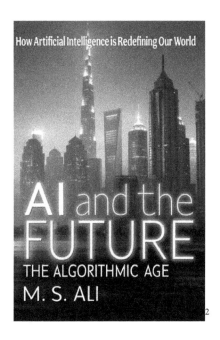

This book is a comprehensive exploration of Artificial Intelligence (AI) and its profound impact on our present and future. Journey with us into The Algorithmic Age, where we unravel the complexities of this transformative technology and its implications for AI Future assisted by AI with a unique blend of scientific rigor, expository clarity, formal instruction, journalistic flair, descriptive richness, persuasive approach, narrative drive, philosophical depth, epigrammatic wit, inspirational zeal, a touch of humor, and genuine empathy.

Here's what you'll discover:

Foundations of AI: Delve into the evolution of AI, from its nascent stages to the rise of Generative AI and Large Language Models (LLMs).

---

1. https://books2read.com/u/4jvAJZ

2. https://books2read.com/u/4jvAJZ

Grasp the core concepts of Machine Learning, Deep Learning, and Neural Networks, and understand how Algorithms shape our Algorithmic Society.AI in Action: Explore real-world applications of AI across diverse sectors, including AI in Business, AI and Education, AI and Healthcare, and AI and the Economy. Discover how AI-Powered Tools are revolutionizing industries and reshaping our daily lives.Societal Impact: Examine the Impact of AI on Society, including its influence on the future of work, ethical considerations in AI Ethics, and the challenges of AI Governance. We'll also discuss AI Safety, AI Alignment, and the potential for AI Consciousness and AI Creativity.The Future of AI: Engage with thought-provoking discussions on the Future of AI, including the rise of AI Agents and AI Chatbots, the role of AI in National Security, and the need for international collaboration in AI Research and development.Who is this book for?

AI for Beginners: New to AI? No problem! We provide a clear and accessible introduction to the field.AI for Students: Perfect for students seeking a deeper understanding of AI concepts and applications.AI for Professionals: Gain valuable insights into how AI is transforming industries and shaping the future of work.Key Themes:

AI and the Future: A forward-looking perspective on the transformative potential of AI.AI Safety Summit: The importance of global cooperation in ensuring the safe and responsible development of AI.AI Regulation: Navigating the legal and ethical challenges of AI, including AI Law and data privacy.This book is your guide to navigating the complexities of the Algorithmic Age. Join us as we explore the fascinating world of Artificial Intelligence and its implications for our future.

Here's what you'll discover:

Foundations of AI: Delve into the evolution of AI, from its nascent stages to the rise of Generative AI and Large Language Models (LLMs). Grasp the core concepts of Machine Learning, Deep Learning, and Neural Networks, and understand how Algorithms shape our Algorithmic Society.AI in Action: Explore real-world applications of AI across diverse sectors, including AI in Business, AI and Education, AI and Healthcare, and AI and the Economy. Discover how AI-Powered Tools are revolutionizing industries and reshaping our daily lives.Societal Impact: Examine the Impact of AI on Society, including its influence on the future of work, ethical considerations in AI Ethics, and the challenges of AI Governance. We'll also discuss AI Safety, AI Alignment, and the potential for AI Consciousness and AI Creativity.The Future of AI: Engage with thought-provoking discussions on the Future of AI, including the rise of AI Agents and AI Chatbots, the role of AI in National Security, and the need for international collaboration in AI Research and development.Who is this book for?

AI for Beginners: New to AI? No problem! We provide a clear and accessible introduction to the field.AI for Students: Perfect for students seeking a deeper understanding of AI concepts and applications.AI for Professionals: Gain valuable insights into how AI is transforming industries and shaping the future of world.

Read more at desertparticle.com.

Also by M.S. Ali

Celestial Wonders
Celestial Secrets - Unlocking the Universe
Our Cosmic Neighborhood - A Tour of Our Galactic Backyard
Beyond the Visible: The Search for Dark Matter
Quantum Curiosities: A Journey Into the Heart of the Quantum World

Wonders of Chemistry
The Green Chemistry Revolution: The Way to a Sustainable Future to a
Sustainable Future

Standalone
AI and the Future: The Algorithmic Age
Quantum Computing for All
The Kitchen Alchemist: The Science of Flavor
Dust to Efficiency: Optimizing Baghouse Operations in Limestone
Calcining
Earth's Tipping Point: Navigating the Anthropocene
The Rise of Autonomous AI: AI's new Dawn
Mind in Motion: AI Robotics for the Curious Creator

Watch for more at desertparticle.com.

About the Author

M.S. Ali is a visionary author revolutionizing science and technology and human understanding by making complex scientific ideas accessible and engaging for modern learners. M.S. Ali leverages the power of AI to synthesize research into compelling narratives, creating books that are both scientifically accurate and captivating.

Read more at desertparticle.com.

About the Publisher

About the publisher: This publisher specializes in a diverse range of educational and engaging content leveraging the cutting-edge AI technologies, focusing on the advancement of knowledge in science and technology, the imaginative worlds of science fiction, and the practical skill development offered by their English speaking course books.

www.ingramcontent.com/pod-product-compliance
Lightning Source LLC
LaVergne TN
LVHW051605050326
832903LV00033B/4370